T0329431

MACAULAY

MACAULAY

A LECTURE
DELIVERED AT CAMBRIDGE
ON AUGUST 10, 1900
IN CONNEXION WITH THE SUMMER MEETING
OF UNIVERSITY EXTENSION STUDENTS

BY

Sir RICHARD C. JEBB M.P.

REGIUS PROFESSOR OF GREEK AND FELLOW OF TRINITY
COLLEGE IN THE UNIVERSITY OF CAMBRIDGE.

PUBLISHED BY REQUEST

CAMBRIDGE:
AT THE UNIVERSITY PRESS.

1900

CAMBRIDGE
UNIVERSITY PRESS

University Printing House, Cambridge CB2 8BS, United Kingdom

Published in the United States of America by Cambridge University Press, New York

Cambridge University Press is part of the University of Cambridge.

It furthers the University's mission by disseminating knowledge in the pursuit of education, learning and research at the highest international levels of excellence.

www.cambridge.org
Information on this title: www.cambridge.org/9781107418745

First published 1900
First paperback edition 2014

A catalogue record for this publication is available from the British Library

ISBN 978-1-107-41874-5 Paperback

MACAULAY.

VISITORS to Trinity College will remember
that, on the north side of the Old Court, a
flagged pathway runs along the wall of the
Chapel. There, some seventy-eight years ago,
on almost any morning in the Long Vacation, a
young man might have been seen walking, book
in hand. His appearance has been described by
a College contemporary, Winthrop Mackworth
Praed. A short, manly figure, marvellously upright, with a bad neckcloth, and one hand in
his waistcoat pocket; with that face of which
Thomas Carlyle, observing it in repose, once
said, 'I noticed the homely Norse features that

J.   I

you find everywhere in the Western Isles, and I thought to myself, "Well, anyone can see that you are a good honest sort of fellow, made out of oatmeal!"' But it was a face, too, which, in Praed's words, bore an expression of great power, and of great good humour. This young man, you would have learned, was Mr Thomas Babington Macaulay, Bachelor of Arts. And that pathway in the Old Court was the spot, as Sir George Trevelyan says, 'where, in his failing years, he specially loved to renew the feelings of the past.' 'Some there are,' he adds, 'who can never revisit it without the fancy that there, if anywhere, his dear shade must linger.'

The historian's father, Zachary Macaulay, was a son of the manse, a Presbyterian who inherited much of the stern spirit of the Scottish Covenanters, a man who, as manager of an estate in Jamaica, had seen for himself the miseries of the negroes, and who was afterwards associated with Wilberforce and Henry Thornton in steadfast effort for the abolition of slavery. Zachary

married, in 1799, Miss Selina Mills, the daughter
of a member of the Society of Friends, who lived
at Bristol. Their eldest child, the historian, was
born in 1800, on October 25,—St Crispin's Day,
and the anniversary, as he loved to remember, of
Agincourt. In the lines written after his rejec-
tion at Edinburgh in 1847, Macaulay says,—

> 'I slumbered, and in slumber saw once more
> A room in an old mansion, long unseen';

that mansion was Rothley Temple, in Leicester-
shire, where he was born ; the seat of his uncle,
Mr Thomas Babington, from whom he derived
his Christian names. At thirteen he was sent to
a private school at Little Shelford, near Cambridge. The best excuse for his now proverbial
phrase, 'every schoolboy knows,' is the amazing
precocity of his own childhood. Before he was
fifteen, he could compare the merits of Boc-
caccio with those of Chaucer, to the advantage
of the former. His memory was already as
wonderful as in later life. At eighteen he went
to Trinity College, Cambridge, where he lived

first in the central part of Bishop's Hostel, and afterwards in rooms between the Great Gate and the Chapel. Among his friends were Derwent Coleridge and Henry Nelson Coleridge, Praed, the poet Moultrie, and the brilliant Charles Austin, who converted him from Toryism to Whiggism,—a process on which Mr Gladstone has remarked that Whigs are usually born, not made. He twice gained the medal for English verse; won the Craven Scholarship, but failed to obtain mathematical honours— indeed, he seems to have regarded every mathematical proposition as an open question, a theme for lively debate. In 1824 he was elected a Fellow of Trinity. In April, 1825, his article on Milton appeared in the *Edinburgh Review*, and he sprang into literary fame. In 1826 he was called to the Bar. Lord Lyndhurst, in 1828, made him a Commissioner of Bankruptcy. In 1830 Lord Lansdowne, struck by his articles on Mill, offered him a seat for Calne in Wiltshire, and he entered the House of Commons.

His first speech on the Reform Bill placed him in the front rank of Parliamentary orators. Mr Gladstone, who entered the House in 1832, says that, whenever Macaulay rose to speak, it was 'a summons like a trumpet-call to fill the benches.'

From 1831 to 1834 his life was extraordinarily full and strenuous. He was appointed a Commissioner, and then Secretary, of the Board of Control, which represented the Crown in its relations with the East India Company. He used to rise at five in the morning to write articles for the *Edinburgh*. He was in a blaze of political and literary success, and a lion of society. No Englishman, says Mr Gladstone, except the younger Pitt and Byron, for a century past had won such immense distinction at so early an age. From 1834 to 1838 he was in India, as legal member of the Supreme Council. He was at the same time Chairman of the Committee of Public Instruction, and drew up the famous minute recommending that the natives of India should be encouraged to study European literature and science. He was also Chairman of the Commission which framed the Penal Code which is still in force throughout British India, and was undoubtedly the chief author of that achievement, which has won such emphatic praise from great lawyers. He returned to England in 1838. In 1839 he became member of Parliament for Edinburgh, and sat till 1847, when he was unseated. From 1839 till the fall of Lord Melbourne's administration in 1841, he was in the Cabinet as Secretary for War; and it was experience of him as a Cabinet Minister that led Lord Melbourne to say, 'Macaulay is so cock-sure about everything.'

In November, 1848, he published the first two volumes of his History. 3000 copies were sold in ten days, and 13,000 in less than three months. The second and third volumes appeared at the end of 1855, and an edition of 25,000 copies went off at once. Meanwhile, in 1852, he had been re-elected member for

Edinburgh, and sat till 1856, when he finally
retired from Parliament. He made some fine
speeches in 1853, but was silent in the House
after that year. In July, 1852, he had been
stricken with heart-disease. 'I became,' he says,
'twenty years older in a week.' Thenceforth
his great physical activity was at an end, and
his tenure of life was precarious. His closing
years were spent at Holly Lodge, Kensington,
whither he had removed, in 1856, from his
chambers in the Albany. There he lived, happy
in his studies, and, as Trevelyan says, a classic
in his own lifetime. In 1857 he was raised to
the Peerage. He died suddenly and peacefully
at Holly Lodge on Dec. 28, 1859, aged fifty-
nine years and two months; and on Jan. 9,
1860, he was laid to rest in Poets' Corner in
Westminster Abbey. His career, from youth
to the close, had been one of almost unbroken
happiness and prosperity. As Mr Gladstone
has well said, 'Full-orbed he was seen above
the horizon; and full-orbed, after thirty-five

years of constantly emitted splendour, he sank below it.'

When the fame of a writer in his lifetime has been not only high but popular, a reaction often sets in after his death; the few avenge themselves on the many. It was so with Pope and with Byron. It was so, for a time, and in a measure, with Macaulay. In the sixties and the seventies it was not uncommon to hear him described as a mere rhetorician. Then there was a superfine criticism, whose own affectations often jarred on a sound taste, that pronounced his style detestable. But, as an Italian proverb says, Time is a good fellow; and things have settled down. Scholars have recognised that Macaulay was a most indefatigable and conscientious student; the world at large still holds that he is a brilliant and fascinating writer. He has passed, without serious scathe, through the ordeal of much criticism, both broad and minute. And at the present day there are at least some readers who can see his greatness as a literary artist even more clearly than it was seen by his contemporaries.

His chief monument is the History of England. It is only a fragment, though it is a colossal fragment. Macaulay's original design was to write the history of England from the accession of James II in 1685 to the death of George IV in 1830, a period of 145 years. But he had not adequately realised the scale of treatment which his conception of history demanded. It was his aim to make the past a living reality to his readers, and to invest historical facts with all, or more than all, the interest of fiction. His brilliant success was largely due to the artistic use of infinite detail in narrative and in the portrayal of character. But, as he soon found when he began to write, this method required vast space. He cannot fairly be charged with diffuseness in the History, except, perhaps, in some cases where he develops a general statement with redundant illustration. On the other hand, he often condenses into a

few words or sentences the results of wide
reading and laborious research.   A careful study
of almost any chapter will show that, relatively
to the mass of particulars which he communi-
cates, his style is, on the whole, compact.   But
even a greater conciseness of language could not
have materially reduced the amount of room
which his plan, by its very nature, demanded.
He had hoped that five volumes would cover
about 36 years, and bring him to the beginning
of Sir Robert Walpole's administration in 1721.
That calculation was completely upset.   The
first two volumes, published in 1849, bring us
only to the acceptance of the Crown by William
and Mary in 1688.   The third and fourth
volumes, published in 1855, bring us to the
Peace of Ryswick in 1697.   No further portion
of the History appeared in his lifetime.   In 1861,
about two years after his death, a fifth volume
was given to the world, edited by his sister,
Lady Trevelyan.   It contains so much of the
continuation as had been revised and transcribed

by Macaulay, carrying the narrative down to 1701. Besides this, the historian had left his first rough sketch of the last two months of William's reign : and from this his sister deciphered, with some difficulty, the account of William's death, which makes some seven pages of print. Now it may readily be granted that the critical years just before and just after the Revolution of 1688 required treatment on an ampler scale than would have been requisite in some later parts of the historian's great task. Still, it is evident that, unless the method was to be radically changed, some thirty or forty volumes, at the least, would have been required to carry the story down to 1830 ; and that, even if the writer, instead of dying at fifty-nine, had lived to a very advanced age, he could not have hoped to reach the goal. If, however, he had been spared for another ten or fifteen years, and had left us perhaps ten or twelve instead of five volumes, the effect of his work, as a masterpiece of literary art, would have been greatly enhanced.

The portion which we possess has been compared by an eloquent critic to the unfinished cathedral of Beauvais, where 'the ornate and soaring choir wants the balance of a majestic nave,' and a great example of French Gothic is deprived of its proper rank by mere incompleteness. It is but bare justice to Macaulay to remember that the new mode of treatment which his genius devised, and the gifts which enabled him to use it with such signal effect, would undoubtedly have been still more impressive, if we could have seen them applied over a larger tract of history.

What are the principal criticisms which have been directed against Macaulay's conception of history, or against particular traits in that splendid, though fragmentary, embodiment of his ideal which he has left to us? In the first place, it has been objected to Macaulay that he is a stranger to the methods and to the spirit of what has been called the critical school of history. He is a picturesque narrator, but

not, in the sense of that school, a scientific
historian. The critical school, which may be
said to date from the end of the last century,
sprang ultimately from a new perception of
complexity in the structure of society, and
was stimulated by the development of political
economy as a systematic study. It aims at
examining the phenomena of the past, no less
than those of the present, by methods which
make some approach to scientific precision,—
so far, that is, as the subject-matter allows,—
and which demand, as a primary condition,
a thorough verification of documents, and of
all obtainable evidence. The critical historian
desires more especially to know how one stage
of society has in past times been developed
out of another; to inquire how far laws of
organic growth can be traced in the development of the human mind and of civilised life;
to see how institutions have been evolved.
Generally, he seeks to classify details under
principles, and to refer effects to causes. Now

Macaulay, it has been complained, scarcely attempts to do any of these things. He tells his story brilliantly, he entertains us, he delights our imagination, or stirs our emotions; but he does not appeal to our reason, he does not enlighten us. For instance, he depicts vividly the temper of the Stuart Kings, the feelings and sufferings of their devoted adherents, but he does not trace the ideas and principles out of which the belief in Divine right, as then held, had grown. He nowhere summarizes, in clear outline, the successive stages of the struggle between Crown and Parliament in the Stuart period. He has much to tell us about the prelates and clergy of those days, but he does not explain how the Church of England had come to be what it then was. In his first chapter, he epitomizes English history from Saxon times without once naming Simon de Montfort, and omits to trace the growth of the English Constitution. Again, it is objected that his lack of the true historical spirit appears in his habit of contrasting the England of the past, to its disadvantage, with the England of the present. The scientific historian, it is said, has nothing to do with the question whether the past is better or worse than the present; his business is simply to tell us what the past was, and how it came to be such. This broad disparagement of Macaulay, on the ground that he is not of the critical school, belongs to that species of censure which consists in blaming a man because he is not somebody else. It is quite true that Macaulay is not of the critical school. It is also true that there have been eminent historians of the critical school who could not, without flattery, be described as powerful or picturesque narrators, or as persons gifted, in any notable degree, with the faculty of making the past live before the minds of their readers. The Muse of History is the queen of a varied realm; and various gifts may be brought to her shrine. Macaulay brought his gift, a sterling and valuable one of its kind;

why need we quarrel with him, because it is not precisely the same gift which would be brought by a disciple of the critical school? If it be urged that the latter is that which a superior person would prefer, we may acquiesce, yet still deny that the other tribute should be excluded. It may be granted that Macaulay would have been a still greater historian than he is, if he had possessed more aptitude for speculative thought,—if his mind had been more philosophic; but the fact that he was not a philosopher is no reason for denying that he was, in his own way, a great historian.

In addition to this general defence, there is something more to be said as to that much-criticized habit of his, the habit of disparaging the past in comparison with the present. It is a habit which is rendered more irritating to many readers by the circumstance that those glories of the present which he extols are so largely the glories of material progress. He exults in the new Manchester and Liverpool as compared with the old ; he points triumphantly to the villas of modern Cheltenham and Tunbridge Wells ;—indeed, the peculiar elation with which the thought of villas often seems to inspire him has been regarded by some æsthetic persons as a very climax of unabashed Philistinism. And it may be frankly allowed that there is something rather trying in Macaulay's perpetual optimism,—the optimism which seems to assume that our country is ever growing wiser and better in proportion as it can show more villas, more steam-engines, more material power and prosperity in every form. This pervading tone is one of the things which Matthew Arnold had in view when he described Macaulay as 'the great apostle of the Philistines.' The tone is indeed one which is apt to jar on any thoughtful reader, even though he be not particularly fastidious ; because it sounds like the utterance of one who undervalues the spiritual side of human life. But let us be just to Macaulay here also. Let us ask how far this

J. 2

tone was rendered natural by the circumstances of the time in which he lived; and also how it is related to his aim as a historian.

At the time of Macaulay's birth, in 1800, England might, no doubt, have been described as a free country relatively to most others; but representative government and political freedom still bore, even in England, a very restricted meaning. At Macaulay's death, in 1859, England was already a free country in the full modern sense. And meanwhile the social condition of the country had been transformed. Macaulay had seen, in his early or middle manhood, the passage of the Reform Bill, the creation of representative municipalities, the extinction of the barbarities which had disgraced the Criminal Law, the repeal of the Corn Laws, the removal of Roman Catholic disabilities, the abolition of the oppressive stamp on newspapers, the institution of the penny post, the application of steam-power to locomotion on land and sea, the introduction of the electric telegraph. The point to observe is that, in Macaulay's time, great strides in material progress had been co-incident with a great and very real elevation of intellectual and moral standards in the nation at large. There had been a marked national advance in the sense of justice, in the sentiments of humanity, in the recognition of rights and duties, in the comprehension of freedom, in the spirit of law and order, in the concord and sympathy between different social classes. It was natural for Macaulay's generation, and it was their habit, closely to associate this mental and moral improvement with the material pro-gress made during the same period; and to a certain extent they were right. When Macaulay pointed exultingly to the fact that Manchester could support twenty coachmakers, or that the shipping registered at the port of Liverpool amounted to nearly half-a-million tons, we should in fairness remember that his intention was not merely to glorify material prosperity as such, but rather to indicate a progress in the whole welfare of the country of which these things were to him the striking outward signs. On the ear of our generation, these pæans of Macaulay's fall with a somewhat depressing effect; they may even be repellent to us; for we have learned to discount some of the expectations of our fathers: we know that material progress has its seamy side; and we know that a vast growth of material prosperity and luxury can lead to a pernicious race for wealth which may become a danger to the highest interests of a nation. But for us to be angry with Macaulay for his tone about these things is as if an elderly man, who had outlived some of his hopes, should resent the sanguine exuberance of youth.

And there is a further point to be observed. The contrasts which Macaulay loves to draw between the seventeenth century and the nineteenth are connected with his special aim as a historian. His constant endeavour was to make the past live again before his reader's mind.

But no one knew better than he the misleading power of names. For instance, when the average man reads about London, he naturally thinks of the nineteenth century London which he knows. It was essential for Macaulay's purpose to make such a reader comprehend that the London of the Stuarts was quite a different sort of place. And he does this, not only by direct description, but by contrasting the old with the new. Any one who examines the History will find that a large proportion of his eulogies on the England of his own day occur under such conditions. True to his love of antithesis, he magnifies the present in order that his reader may receive a more vivid impression of the difference between the present and the past.

Thus far I have spoken of the criticisms which object to Macaulay that he is not a scientific historian, and that he sins against the historical spirit. I pass now to a criticism, which, though still of large range, relates not to his method as such, but to his treatment of his chosen subject. This is, in brief, the charge of partisanship; he has been accused of a strong Whig bias. No one would deny that a historian, who has faithfully examined the evidence, and who faithfully reports it, is entitled to draw his own inferences from it, and to express his own opinion. The impartiality demanded from the historian, as from the judicial bench, is not neutrality. What Edmund Burke said of representatives in Parliament is equally true of historians; they owe to the public not only their knowledge but their judgment. Macaulay makes no secret of his convictions and his sympathies. The question is, have his opinions deflected his narrative from the course of truth and fairness? It has never been shown that they have done so in regard to any of the larger and more important issues with which he deals. He is, indeed, uncompromising in his severity towards the house of Stuart; and it is not surprising that his History should have given offence wherever a sentimental Jacobitism survived. But such severity is not peculiar to English Whigs; an equally unfavourable view of the Stuarts has been taken by foreign historians, such as Ranke and Gneist. It is true, no doubt, that William of Orange is Macaulay's hero. There was no evil that the Jacobites of 1688, and of a later age also, were not ready to speak or to believe about William; but has Macaulay been convicted by any unprejudiced and candid critic, either of exaggerating William's merits in any material respect, or of suppressing a misdeed with which he was chargeable? There is perhaps only one case, of any gravity, in which such an accusation has been effectively brought against Macaulay. He holds that King William was not morally responsible for the massacre of the Macdonalds at Glencoe; because, says Macaulay, though the King signed the military order which preceded the massacre, he did not comprehend the local situation; he imagined that these Macdonalds were a mere gang of

banditti who were preying on their peaceable
neighbours.   The blemish on William's fame in
this matter is, according to Macaulay, that he
did not afterwards inflict condign punishment
on the real culprit, the Master of Stair.   On
this point the results of later research seem to
be against Macaulay.   It can scarcely be doubted
that William knew pretty well what he was
doing, and sanctioned the deed, in the hope of
striking terror into the rebels.   But let us remember, on the other hand, that Macaulay was
the first English historian who gave Englishmen
any adequate notion of William's place in history.
As Napoleon was a menace to Europe at the
beginning of the 19th century, so was Louis
XIV at the epoch of our Revolution; and
Macaulay rendered only justice to William,—
justice which had never been fully rendered
before,—by exhibiting him as the pilot who
weathered the storm, the champion both of
England and of Europe.   To the Revolution of
1688 Macaulay traced the origin of modern

English liberties,—incomplete though they then were,—and the beginning of a new and more prosperous era for our country. He judged the men of that age, not according as they were Whigs or Tories, but according to the measure in which he believed them to have been honest and upright men, friends of reasonable liberty, loyal to their country. He is always fair to sincere and highminded Tories, such as Lord Nottingham and many more. He can fully appreciate such a non-juror as Jeremy Collier, and he warmly admires the non-juring Bishop Ken. On the other hand, he condemns the Whig persecution of Roman Catholics as strongly as Lingard himself. In fine, Macaulay cannot be justly charged with having allowed his strong personal predilections or sympathies to distort his general views of history.

But there remains yet another category of criticisms. It is alleged that in the History he has been guilty of injustice to certain individuals, or to certain classes of persons. Probably no historian has ever escaped, or ever will escape, this kind of accusation. It will be remembered that William Penn, the founder of Pennsylvania, enjoyed the intimate confidence of James II, and had great influence at Court. One of the worst scandals of a reign in which justice was dispensed by such men as Jeffreys was the sale of pardons, for the profit of courtiers and favourites. Following Sir James Mackintosh, Macaulay assumed, on the strength of a letter written by Sunderland to a Mr Penne, that William Penn had been the agent in one peculiarly infamous sale of pardons. The Society of Friends promptly took up the defence of the famous Quaker. Among his vindicators was the late Right Hon. W. E. Forster. They contended that Macaulay had confused William Penn with a low adventurer named George Penne, who certainly acted as a go-between in such bargains. Mr Forster and four other Quakers even went as a deputation to Macaulay at his chambers in the Albany, and laid their

case before him.   He harangued them in reply,
and remained under the pleasing illusion that
he had converted them ; whereas they went
away simmering with quiet indignation.   I cannot go into the controversy ; but I wish to
emphasize one point.   Macaulay's conduct in
the matter has been described, even by so
candid and generous a critic as Mr Gladstone,
in terms which might seem to imply that he
simply ignored the Quakers' arguments, and
curtly refused all redress.   This is not the fact.
In revising his fifth chapter, where the incident
occurs, Macaulay added a very long foot-note,
equivalent to some five pages, in which he fully
discusses the theory about George Penne advanced by the Quakers, and gives in ample
detail his reasons for adhering to his original
statement.   Macaulay has also been accused of
injustice to Marlborough ; but that charge at
once breaks down.   There is no doubt that
Marlborough, who, like several other statesmen
of the time, tried to stand well both with William

and with James, sent news to the exile at St Germains of the English intention to attack the French port of Brest. I shall mention only one other case. Nothing in Macaulay's History gave wider or deeper offence than the passage about the position of the Anglican clergy in the latter part of the 17th century. He says that the Reformation had completely changed the place of clergymen in society, and that, in the reigns of Charles II and James II, 'for every one who made the figure of a gentleman, ten were mere menial servants.' That is pretty strong; but he adds an assertion that the marriages formed by the clergy were ordinarily such as suited that condition, and not infrequently were very much worse. The late Professor Churchill Babington, of St John's College, Cambridge, conclusively refuted this libel in an essay which he published in 1849, very soon after the appearance of Macaulay's first two volumes. Mr Gladstone, writing in the *Quarterly Review*, for April, 1876, recognises Babington's essay as convincing, adopts it as his principal authority, and reinforces its conclusions. There is no reason to doubt that the position of some clergymen, especially of domestic chaplains in some country houses,— though not in the best,—was often bad enough ; but it may be regarded as certain that Macaulay went very wide of the mark when he affirmed that nine-tenths of the Anglican Clergy were in that position of social inferiority which he de- picts. His sweeping statement on this subject is the strongest example, perhaps, in all his writings of a danger to which he was exposed by an active fancy which could always draw on the ready stores of a prodigious memory. If Macaulay had been challenged in conversation about this account of the Anglican Clergy, we can conjecture, even from his own text, how he would have replied. He would have poured forth a torrent of citations from the literature, chiefly the lighter literature, of that age ; he would have quoted Fletcher's 'Scornful Lady,' Vanbrugh's 'Relapse,' Shadwell's 'Lancashire

Witches,' Swift's 'Directions to Servants,' and
twenty other pieces where clergymen are the
objects of scornful allusion; and he would then
have held that he had triumphantly proved his
point. But it is obvious that the satirists and
comic dramatists of the Restoration are not
precisely the sources to which we should go for
a dispassionate view of the social position occupied by the Anglican Clergy, as a class, at
a period when the prevailing tone of Whitehall
and of London was not very religious, and so
far as it was religious, was anything rather than
Anglican. Nor is the evidence of comic drama
and of satire valuably strengthened by such
a pamphlet as Eachard's—one of Macaulay's
chief authorities—on the 'Causes of Contempt
of the Clergy'; still less by that subtler and
mightier voice from the time of Queen Anne,
the voice of a great but embittered genius, the
Irish Dean of St Patrick's.

I have now attempted to indicate the general
nature, and the scope, of the principal criticisms

which have been made on Macaulay's History.
It will be seen that the nett results do not con-
stitute any serious deduction from the merits
which are now universally recognised in that
great work. It is no longer pretended that
Macaulay, as a historian, is shallow or superficial. Students who have been over the same
ground have borne witness to the thoroughness
and fidelity with which he has examined and
sifted his materials. Beneath that brilliant style,
which a criticism, itself shallow and superficial,
sometimes assumed to be incompatible with
soundness, such students have recognised a laborious and conscientious diligence which the
dullest and driest of writers could not have
surpassed. Among all historians, Macaulay is
supreme in narrative power; and it is well to
note, however briefly, some of the qualities to
which he owes that pre-eminence. First, he
knows in the utmost detail the whole biography
of every considerable person whom he introduces, and the history of every important place

or building. Secondly, his absolute mastery of
material is joined to a fine artistic sense. This
enables him, again and again, to light up his
pictures with little touches which add wonder-
fully to their vividness. Take, for example, his
description of that moment when King James,
after his first attempt to fly the country, was
virtually a prisoner in his own palace at Whitehall. ' In the evening '—Macaulay writes—'news
came that the Dutch had occupied Chelsea and
Kensington. The King, however, prepared to
go to rest as usual. The Coldstream Guards
were on duty at the palace. They were commanded by William, Earl of Craven, an aged
man, who, more than fifty years before, had
been distinguished in war and love, who had
led the forlorn hope at Creutznach with such
courage that he had been patted on the shoulder
by the great Gustavus, and who was believed to
have won from a thousand rivals the heart of
the unfortunate Queen of Bohemia. Craven
was now in his eightieth year; yet time had not

tamed his spirit. It was past ten o'clock when he was informed that three battalions of the Prince's foot, mingled with some troops of horse, were pouring down the long avenue of St James's Park, with matches lighted, and in full readiness for action. Count Solmes, who commanded the foreigners, said that his orders were to take military possession of the posts round Whitehall, and exhorted Craven to retire peaceably. Craven swore that he would rather be cut to pieces ; but when the King, who was undressing himself, learned what was passing, he forbade the stout old soldier to attempt a resistance which must have been ineffectual.'

Observe how Macaulay heightens the impression of the veteran Craven's gallantry by that passing allusion which carries us back to the far-off days of the Thirty Years' War, to the forlorn hope at Creutznach, and evokes for a moment the shade of the great Gustavus, approving the heroism of the young English captain ! It is only one instance of a power

which Macaulay has always at command.   It is
this artistic power in applying minute touches
which led Mr Gladstone to say of Macaulay's
descriptions that 'the finest cabinet pictures of
Holland are almost his only rivals'; and which
suggested to Mr Cotter Morison,—no unqualified
admirer,—the comparison with 'a richly deco-
rated Gothic porch, in which every stone is
curiously carved, and yet does its duty in bear-
ing the weight of the mighty arch as well as if
it were perfectly plain.'   And as with persons,
so also with places.   Read Macaulay's narrative
of the siege of Londonderry, and see how it is
instinct with minute local knowledge.   Or, to
take an instance on a smaller scale, consider
how, in speaking of Monmouth's death, he inci-
dentally characterises the place where he is
buried,—St Peter's Chapel in the Tower :—' In
truth there is no sadder spot on the earth than
that little cemetery.   Death is there associated,
not as in Westminster Abbey or St Paul's, with
genius and virtue, with public veneration and

imperishable renown; not, as in our humblest churches and churchyards, with everything that is most endearing in social and domestic charities; but with whatever is darkest in human nature and in human destiny; with the savage triumph of implacable enemies; with the inconstancy, the ingratitude, the cowardice of friends; with all the miseries of fallen greatness and of blighted fame.' Space would fail me to give more instances; you will find them in every chapter. But I must quote the admirable tribute paid to this quality of Macaulay's work by one who was himself a great literary artist,—by Thackeray :—

'Take'—he says—'at hazard any three pages of the Essays, or the History, and shimmering below the stream of the narrative, as it were, you, an average reader, see one, two, three, a half-score of allusions to other historic facts, characters, literature, poetry, with which you are acquainted. Why is that epithet used? Whence is that simile drawn? How does he manage, in two or three words, to paint an individual, or to indicate a landscape? Your neighbour, who has *his* reading,...shall detect more points, allusions, happy touches, indicating not only the prodigious memory and vast learning of this master, but the wonderful industry, the honest, humble, previous toil of this great scholar. He reads twenty books to write a sentence; he travels a hundred miles to make a line of description.'

This artistic command of detail is, however, only one of the qualities which go to make up Macaulay's excellence in narrative. Another and larger one, to which this is subservient, is the power of telling a story dramatically. No writer of fiction, not even the greatest, has excelled Macaulay in this art. Any one who wishes for an example of it may turn to the ninth chapter of the History, and read the passage—it is too long to quote—in which Macaulay describes the flight of the Princess Anne, in company with Sarah Lady Churchill, from Whitehall, at the moment when her father,

King James, was retreating from Salisbury on London.   And if the reader wishes to heighten his perception by a foil, then let him turn to the pages of Hume, and see how the same story is told there.   But, beyond this dramatic power in the handling of a single story, Macaulay has another gift, which is more distinctively his own. It is the power of managing a complex narrative, in which a number of secondary streams, or affluents, are contributory to the main current of events.   Take, as one large example of this power, the whole account of James's reign in the first two volumes of the History.   The *dramatis personae* are numerous, the scene frequently changes, there is a multitude of minor episodes, but the unity of effect is complete. As some one has said of it, at whatever point you stand, you seem to be opposite the centre of the picture.   This could have been achieved only by a writer of literary genius ; but it was not achieved without great and incessant labour. Macaulay   thought   nothing   of   recasting   or rewriting whole chapters in order to obtain a completely harmonious result. There is a passage in his journal which admits us to the secrets of his study, and permits us to hear him thinking aloud over his work:—'This is a tough chapter'—he says. 'To make the narrative flow along as it ought, each part naturally springing from that which precedes, is not easy. What trouble these few pages have cost me! The great object is that they may read as if they had been spoken off, and flow as easily as table-talk.' Let any one, in reading Macaulay's History, carefully note the transitions when the narrative passes from one part of the field to another, and he will appreciate the art which conceals art. These transitions, which seem so easy and natural, are often, in reality, very bold. And the same art may be observed in his mode of returning from a digression: he never seems to have digressed; and he brings us back with a quickened interest to the highway of his narrative.

Such are some of the more evident qualities which help to give Macaulay his supre-
macy as a narrator; though there is also in
his gift much that is as indefinable as it is
incommunicable, much that eludes and tran-
scends analysis, and of which we can only say
that it distinguishes him from other men. It
would, however, be doing scant justice to the
History if we should dwell only, or even prin-
cipally, on its merits of form. Reference has
already been made to the solid and laborious
studies on which it is based. But it is much more
than an achievement of learning and of style.
The moral tone which pervades the History
is manly and sound. It condones no deed of
treachery or cruelty; it has no tolerance for
hypocrisy or pretence; it also awards praise
without stint to fortitude, to honest effort, to
self-sacrifice, wherever they are found. There
is no attempt to win a cheap and spurious credit
for originality by the poor device of white-
washing bad characters, or of detracting from

generally acknowledged merit. A robust judgment, an honest and independent spirit, can be
felt throughout the work; it inculcates a respect
for civil justice, and it is animated by a generous
love of constitutional freedom.

The History, it should be remembered, is
the literary work by which Macaulay would
have wished that posterity should judge him.
The reading public will, indeed, always associate
him with the Essays as much as with the
History; but this is not what he himself would
have desired. In the preface to the first collected
edition of the Essays, he says :—' The author
of these Essays is so sensible of their defects
that he repeatedly refused to let them appear
in a form which might seem to indicate that he
thought them worthy of a permanent place in
English literature.' He consented at last only
because they had been published in America,
and he felt bound to protect the proprietors
of the ' Edinburgh Review.' Of the twenty-
seven Essays whose publication he reluctantly

sanctioned, the earliest, that on Milton, was written at the age of twenty-five; the latest, —the second Essay on the Elder Pitt,—at the age of forty-four. All thus belong to the most vigorous period of his life, and almost all were written amidst the pressure of occupations and engagements, political, official, and social. In republishing them, he made no attempt to remodel any one of them. His revision was limited to removing those blemishes which, at the time of their first appearance, had been due to unavoidable haste. To the average reader, all the Essays alike appear brilliant, because all alike exhibit the splendours of his style. But to any one who examines the quality of the matter and of the thought, the most striking thing about the Essays, taken altogether, is perhaps the wide differences of merit between the best and the worst. Macaulay himself was doubtless fully conscious of this, and it must have been one of his reasons for demurring to a collected edition. Among the best of the Essays, as most critics would probably agree, are those on Sir William Temple, Hallam's Constitutional History, the Elder Pitt, Clive, and Warren Hastings. Large, indeed, is the interval, in respect of solid merit, which separates these from such Essays as those on Burleigh and his times, Ranke's history of the Popes, and Bacon. The last-named, in which Macaulay seems to contemn all speculative thought, and declares that the first cobbler was preferable to Seneca, has certainly damaged his reputation as a thinker more than anything that he ever wrote; while certain of his imputations upon Bacon's character has elicited the elaborate refutation by Spedding. Several other Essays, of an intermediate class in general merit, are also open to serious criticism. He greatly underrated Horace Walpole's capacity. What is much more extraordinary, he failed to perceive that Boswell, whom he treats as a dunce and a fool, shows a marvellous dramatic faculty in his presentation of Johnson. Some of the other pieces are open to objections hardly less grave.

But, when all has been said, it remains true that Macaulay gave a new life and meaning to the historical Essay. He made it a vehicle through which thousands of people, who would never have read history at all, have acquired in a pleasurable way some acquaintance with great characters and events. These essays are probably the best of their kind in Europe. And there can be no doubt that they will live. Only it is much to be desired that, when they are used for purposes of education, students should be warned against the errors which many of them contain. On a higher level than any but the very best of the Essays, stand those five biographies which Macaulay wrote for the ' Encyclopædia Britannica,'—those of Atterbury, Bunyan, Goldsmith, Johnson, and the younger Pitt. All these are mature and careful pieces of work, quieter and more restrained in style

than the Essays, but hardly less attractive.
They show Macaulay as a master of artistic
condensation.　Taking into account their merits
both of matter and of form, we should be safe in
affirming that, as a writer of short biographies,
Macaulay has not been surpassed, if he has
been equalled, by any English writer.　The
life of the younger Pitt, in particular, calls for
unqualified admiration.　It was written in the
January of 1859, the year of his death ; and
he never wrote anything better.　It is a sample
of what he could have done in the History if
he had reached that period, and it must en-
hance our regret that the History remained
a fragment.

From the History and the Essays, I turn
to ask a general question which they suggest.
We have already seen some of the characteristics of Macaulay's historical method, and of
his power in narrative.　But what was the
nature of that attribute which has been generally
regarded as the most original and distinctive

thing about him,—his famous *style*? When, at twenty-five, he sent his essay on Milton to the 'Edinburgh Review,' Jeffrey, the editor, in acknowledging it, said, 'The more I think, the less I can conceive, where you picked up that style.' Earlier than that, while he was still at Trinity College, he wrote an essay on the conduct and character of William III ; and there we already find the same style—not quite full-blown, but with all the essential traits well-marked. It was not a laboriously acquired manner, it was his natural mode of utterance.

Now, what are its essential characteristics?

The first, the dominant one, is the close relation which it exhibits between the written and the spoken word. It is the style of a born orator. There is in it a sustained vivacity and rapidity which at once declare this. Macaulay imparts to written speech much of the impetus and the swing of oratory. This is by no means the same thing as to write rhetorically. The epithet 'rhetorical' may doubtless be given to Macaulay's style as a whole, though with different shades of meaning in different places; but there could be no greater mistake than to say that Macaulay, as a stylist, is merely a rhetorician. A mere rhetorician, however skilful or brilliant, could not have reached Macaulay's higher effects. Rhetoric is an art of diction and composition. Oratory may, and usually does, owe something to rhetoric, but implies much more; it implies an inward fire, a glow and movement of the spirit, a powerful and sincere emotion which the speaker can communicate to the hearers; and in all Macaulay's greatest passages we are conscious of these things. When his style is at its best and highest, we can recognize in it the quality which Cicero, in a well-known sentence, ascribes to eloquence: 'It is with eloquence as with flame; movement excites it, matter feeds it, and it brightens as it burns.' This oratorical character of Macaulay's style may be illustrated by one of its most salient and familiar traits : I mean, his habit of placing very short sentences between his longer periods. This has sometimes been regarded as a mere literary artifice, and critics have complained that it has a jerky effect. It is true, no doubt, that Macaulay sometimes overdid it ; but I am not now asking whether, in itself, this trait is, in a literary view, good ; my point is that it is a trait of oratory. Take the speeches of almost any great orator, and you will find a similar, though perhaps less abundant, use of short sentences, in alternation with long periods. Such short sentences are not merely pauses for breath ; they are not merely deliberate efforts to vary the rhythm and arrest the ear : they are dictated, if one may say so, by the oratorical instinct ; such alternations of the long and the short sentence correspond with a certain surging and subsidence of thought and feeling in the orator's mind.

Next,—it follows from this fundamental characteristic of Macaulay's style that it cannot

be adequately judged by a short specimen,—
by a selection of sentences or even of para-
graphs. There are some of the more delicate
and exquisite styles that can be so judged.
An extract of very moderate compass might
serve to convey a fairly just idea of Landor's
style, for instance, or of Newman's, or even
of Ruskin's. But it is not so with Macaulay.
As well could you have estimated the oratory
of Gladstone or of Bright by two minutes of
their speech. As an orator must be judged by
a completed utterance, so Macaulay must be
judged by large integral units of his composition, such as whole chapters or essays. Both
the critics and the imitators of his style have
frequently failed to perceive this. An example
may serve to make my meaning clearer.
Macaulay often introduces passages which are,
in the strictest sense of the word, rhetorical,—
possessing, indeed, the highest finish and splendour of which English rhetoric is capable. Such
is the famous description of the scene in West-

minster Hall at the trial of Warren Hastings. We all remember the manner of it:—' There Siddons, in the prime of her majestic beauty, looked with emotion on a scene surpassing all the imitations of the stage. There the historian of the Roman Empire thought of the days when Cicero pleaded the cause of Sicily against Verres, and when, before a Senate which retained some show of freedom, Tacitus thundered against the oppressor of Africa.' That gorgeous description, quoted in an extract, would certainly be a good specimen of Macaulay's *rhetoric*, but it would not convey any just impression of his *style*. The high rhetorical elaboration of that passage is suited to the context, to what precedes, and what is to follow; the rhetoric is not the cold art of the study, but answers to the strong emotion which rises in Macaulay's mind as he comes to the central episode in his thrilling story. Read the essay in its entirety, and you will see how this incidental use of rhetoric is subordinate to a higher energy

J. 4

and a larger inspiration which inform his style as a whole.

Macaulay had a wonderful fulness and variety of knowledge. His vivid imagination, drawing on the immense stores which his prodigious memory held ready for use at any moment, gave him an almost unrivalled command of brilliant illustration. Facts, images, analogies crowded upon his mind whenever he desired to enforce an argument or to embellish a statement. He has himself given us a remarkable account of the process by which this faculty had been fostered and developed. To his sister Margaret (afterwards Mrs Edward Cropper) he said in early manhood: 'My accuracy as to facts I owe to a cause which many men would not confess. It is due to my love of castle-building. The past is in my mind soon constructed into a romance.' He then described how, from childhood, he had lived in the past. 'I am no sooner in the streets, than I am in Greece, in Rome, in the midst of the

French Revolution....A slight fact, a sentence, a word, are of importance in my romance.' Every part of Old London was peopled, for him, by figures from bygone days. Referring again, in 1858, to this life-long habit of day-dreaming, he said :—'I, at least, impute to it a great part of my literary success.' The habit was sometimes a source of error to him, because, as Mr Gladstone and Mr Leslie Stephen have observed, the facts supplied by his memory became coloured by his fancy, especially where questions of character or opinion were concerned. But he was doubtless right when he said that he owed to this habit much of his literary success. In these day-dreams he was always testing his hold upon his vast resources. And it was essential for the effective use of such a style as his that he should have a wide and easy mastery of facts, allusions and images.

Few things in Macaulay's diary are more interesting than some sentences in which he refers to his imitators. 'A new number of the Review. There is an article which is a mocking-bird imitation of me. Somehow or other, the mimic cannot catch the note, but many people would not be able to distinguish.' Again :—' I looked through ——'s two volumes. He is, I see, an imitator of me. But I am a very unsafe model. My manner is, I think, and the world thinks, on the whole a good one; but it is very near to a very bad manner indeed, and those characteristics of my style which are most easily copied are the most questionable.' That is perfectly true, and is a notably good bit of self-criticism. It is easy to imitate, for instance, Macaulay's excessive fondness for an-tithesis ; his love of glowing colours and strong contrasts ; his insensibility to the charm and the value of graduated tones and neutral tints. His manner is often, as he said, very near to a bad one ; but it escapes from being such, and attains to excellence, by dint of just those things which an ordinary imitator cannot reach ; viz., by a true and fine artistic sense for large effects; by an indwelling poetical fire and fancy; by a complete and classical mastery of our language; by an astonishing wealth and felicity of illustration; and, if we consider the movement of his style through entire pieces, by the spirit, the *afflatus*, of a born orator.

Matthew Arnold was unjust to Macaulay's style. Its external characteristic, he said, was 'a hard metallic movement, with nothing of the soft play of life.' By 'the soft play of life' he seems to mean a charm which we find in styles of which the interest is chiefly sub-jective,—that is, dependent on interpretation of a writer's own moods and fancies, when he takes the reader into his confidence. We find it, for instance, in Addison, in Charles Lamb, in De Quincey, or with a graver and more penetrating beauty, in Newman. But there are other styles more especially adapted to the historical presentation of facts, and to the conduct of argument, not as among intimates, but in the forum. Such styles, as distinguished from the others, may be called objective; and in these we do not look for 'the *soft* play of life.' Gibbon's is such a style; Macaulay's is another. It suited his subjects; it also suited his temperament, which, though imaginatively dreamy, was not reflective, and still less introspective. It is a style, of course, which has its limitations; but it has also its own sphere, its own virtues, its own beauty and grandeur; yes, and its own play of life too—but not that which Matthew Arnold calls a *soft* play of life. Then Mr Arnold says that the *internal* characteristic of Macaulay's style is 'a perpetual semblance of hitting the right nail on the head without the reality.' Let us hear how an excellent and witty critic, Mr Herbert Paul, replies to this. 'To say with Matthew Arnold' —Mr Paul writes—'that [Macaulay's style] has the perpetual semblance of hitting the right nail on the head without the reality, is in my judgment absurd. Macaulay habitually hit the right nail on the head, and he did not, as Mr Arnold sometimes did, knock out two tacks in the process.' But Mr Paul adds that, in Macaulay, 'there is always the semblance as well as the reality, and it is the reality without the semblance which charms us in the greatest writers of all.' That is well said. It is quite true that Macaulay often brings down his hammer on his nail with too much of a flourish. He is too exultant. As to this, it may suffice to observe that an author who transfers to literature the vigour and the splendour of oratory inevitably transfers to it also a trait which, in literature, is less pleasing, viz., the orator's triumphant manner of clinching an argument.

As a writer of verse, Macaulay has been variously estimated. Mr Gladstone said : 'His works in verse possess the chief merits of his other works, and are free from their faults.' No fair critic, I think, would deny poetical merit to many passages in the 'Lays of Ancient Rome' : such, for instance, as the falling of the bridge in the lay of 'Horatius,' the description of

the vision which came to the false Sextus, or in
'Virginia,' the dramatic speech of Icilius.　Not
without reminiscences of Scott, Macaulay took
the romantic ballad, and put into it a wholly
different spirit, the civic spirit of ancient Rome.
The vast and enduring popularity of the 'Lays'
does not, indeed, prove that they are poetry,
but it proves that they are heart-stirring.
Macaulay shows in them the same kind of
power which we see in Mr Rudyard Kipling's
best poem—as many people deem it—the 'Re-
cessional'; that is, rhetorical power, kindled
into poetry by the kind of emotion which great
national events or causes stir in poetically-
minded men.　The lines written by Macaulay
after his defeat at Edinburgh in 1847 show real
feeling, and are most brilliant, but they are
rather too rhetorical; and the motive is not
congenial to high poetry—a man's feeling after
an adverse declaration of the poll.　I prefer the
'Sermon in a Churchyard,' a somewhat Byronic
piece which he wrote in 1825; and still more

the 'Epitaph on a Jacobite,'—his best verses,
perhaps,—those beginning,

> 'To my true king I offered free from stain
> Courage and faith ; vain faith and courage vain.'

They show how thoroughly he felt the
nobler and more pathetic side of a cause which,
politically, he detested. But the fact is that he
had not the spiritual subtlety or insight which
belongs to the higher poetry; and this is one
reason why he was ill-fitted for certain branches
of criticism, as he well knew. In 1838 he said
in a letter to Macvey Napier, 'I have never
written a page of criticism on poetry, or the fine
arts, which I would not burn if I had the
power....Such books as Lessing's Laocoon, such
passages as the criticism on Hamlet in Wilhelm
Meister, fill me with wonder and despair.' The
fact that he seems never to have been in
love might also, perhaps, be noted in this context.

It is one of our debts to Sir George
Trevelyan that, instead of knowing Macaulay

only as a writer, we now know him also as a man. Macaulay's was a nature of rare sweetness, purity, and strength. He was affectionate and unselfish ; a devoted son, and that under severe trials; a devoted brother, full of affection, and at need, of self-sacrifice, towards all his kindred. He was free from envy, and from literary vanity. He patiently bore the insolence of people who were among his most regular pensioners. 'That wretched K.' he writes, 'has sent a scurrilous begging-letter in his usual style. He hears that I have made £30,000 by my malignant abuse of good men. Will I not send him some of it?' His liberality to indigent men of letters was unfailing, and almost too unguarded. In all relations of life he was benevolent and chivalrous. The record of his career may be searched in vain for a trace of meanness or cowardice, for an instance of deviation from upright and worthy aims. Moultrie, who had known him from youth, could say of him,—

> 'His heart was pure and simple as a child's,
> Unbreathed on by the world; in friendship warm,
> Confiding, generous, constant.'

Macaulay will be remembered as a historian, a legislator, an orator, a writer of stirring or pathetic verse, a great scholar and a consummate literary artist; but also as a man whose character merited, in the amplest measure, respect, admiration, and love.

Printed in the United States
By Bookmasters